FOR

It May Not Work the Way You Think it Does

WARREN G. LAMB

and

TRUTH IN LOVE BIBLICAL COUNSELING

Forgiveness: It May Not Work the Way You Think it Does
Copyright © 2022 by
Warren G. Lamb and Truth in Love Biblical Counseling

All rights reserved. No portion of this book may be reproduced in any form without permission from the publisher except as permitted by U.S. copyright law.

Forgiveness: It May Not Work the Way You've Been Taught has been adapted from the *Truth in Love Biblical Counseling's "Unbound: Growing Ever-freer in Christ—Second Edition"* curriculum, Lesson Fourteen, "Forgiveness: What It Is; What It Isn't". Copyright © 2008-2022. Used by permission.

All Scripture quotations are taken from the (NASB®) New American Standard Bible®, Copyright © 1960, 1971, 1977, 1995, 2020 by The Lockman Foundation. Used by permission. All rights reserved. www.lockman.org

Cover Photo and photo on dedication page from Shutterstock and used under license from shutterstock.com

ISBN: 979-8-365-50108-9

TILBCC

Truth in Love Biblical Counseling & Training Center
An Auxiliary Ministry of
Truth in Love Fellowship
PO Box 516
Tustin, CA 92781-0516

Printed and bound in
The United States of America

Dedicated to all those who have been made to feel sinful, rebellious, or "less-than" for not being able to "forgive, forget, and move on."

And to those whose misunderstanding of biblical forgiveness has wounded Christ's lambs.

May we better understand what "as God in Christ has forgiven you" truly means and live faithful to it, helping others do the same.

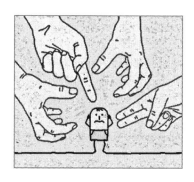

Table of Contents

Introduction 1

The Defective-Hermeneutics Spiral 2

Three Forms of Forgiveness 5

    Judicial Forgiveness 5

    Internal Forgiveness 8

    Relational Forgiveness 10

What About Forgiving Myself? 15

What About Being a Peacemaker? 18

Final Thoughts 20

FORGIVENESS:
It May Not Work the Way You Think it Does

"Be kind to one another, tender-hearted, forgiving one another, just as God in Christ also has forgiven you."
Ephesians 4:32

Introduction

Forgiveness is poorly understood and even more poorly taught in many Christian circles today. A combination of defective hermeneutics (the rules of proper Bible interpretation), bad logic, weaving together incompatible ideas, added to a certain level of emotionalism, and all blended together with one person after another repeating the same misinformation, has created an unbiblical and unhealthy view of forgiveness. This lesson is intended to help you understand forgiveness from God's perspective. We trust it will be a help.

FORGIVENESS: It May Not Work the Way You Think

The Defective-Hermeneutics[1] Spiral

In Psalm 103:12, we read: *"As far as the east is from the west, so far has He removed our transgressions from us."*

In Isaiah 43:25, the Lord is quoted as saying, *"I, even I, am the one who wipes out your transgressions for My own sake, and I will not remember your sins."*

Then, in Hebrews 8:12 (quoting Isaiah 43:25; Jeremiah 31:34; Jeremiah 50:20; and Micah 7:18-19), we read, *"For I will be merciful to their iniquities, and I will remember their sins no more."*

These passages are often conflated and over-extrapolated, and the result is the false doctrine of "Forgive, Forget, and Move On." Because of a misunderstanding of the biblical languages and a weak approach to hermeneutics, we are often taught that the

---

[1] Hermeneutics (her-muh-*NOO*-tiks) is the art and science of Biblical interpretation. There are specific "do's" and "don'ts" that must be followed if we are going to understand the true meaning and significance of God's Word.

phrases "remember no more," and "will not remember," mean that God develops the equivalent of "Divine Amnesia."

In reality, this is not at all the case. Both the Hebrew and the Greek words used in these and comparable passages where the idea of remembering/not remembering is present refer to a "being mindful of," or "mentioning" (and similar concepts).

When this misunderstanding is combined with Philippians 3:13 (where Paul speaks of "forgetting what is behind" — referring to his pedigree and accomplishments, as well as to what others have done to him), taken out of context and misapplied, they arrive at the defective idea that, as Christians, we are to, "Forgive, forget, and move on." As regards forgiveness, nothing could be more unbiblical.

In fact, this false teaching regularly re-traumatizes people and, very often, becomes a stranglehold on a person's ability to escape false guilt and the associated toxic shame

(shame targeted at who a person is, not about what they have done).

It is important that we take hold of God's view of forgiveness and adhere to it if we are to live healthy and free, and become able to walk in authentic, godly forgiveness.

Despite a great deal of misunderstanding and inaccurate teaching in the church regarding forgiveness, we want to leave this session with a clearer understanding of this crucial truth. We need to base our understanding not only on what the Word truly says, but also on what God has Himself demonstrated.

Three Forms of Forgiveness

There are three forms or kinds of forgiveness described in the Bible. One is completely up to God; one is up to us; and one cannot and ought not to happen without a certain amount of work on the part of the offending party.

1. **Judicial Forgiveness:** This is the complete pardon of all sin granted by God that only He can provide to someone when someone personally goes to Him in confession and repentance of their own sin — and no one else's.

Through such repentance and our faith in Christ's atoning sacrifice, God (as the Supreme and Righteous Judge) grants "Judicial Forgiveness." *Everyone* has to go to God on their own to receive this type of forgiveness.

We will never be able to be forgiven for the sins of other people. Thinking that we need to be is part of what causes false guilt, toxic shame, and destructive idolatries in our lives.

Judicial Forgiveness precedes our **Relational Forgiveness** with God and, as we've already said, requires two things on our part: Confession and true repentance (1 John 1:9).

"WORDS MATTER"

Confess: The word translated as "confess" in 1 John 1:9 is a judicial term that means "to be in verbal agreement on the exact nature and character of our wrong." In our judicial system today, there is a similar term used: "allocute," which means "to speak out formally." In practice, when 1 John was written and in American jurisprudence today, this means, "To verbally agree on the exact nature and character of the wrong [crime] without rationalizing, justifying, minimizing, or blameshifting."

Contrite Heart: Apart from a contrite heart, true confession and authentic repentance cannot exist. A contrite heart means the guilty party has a wide-open acceptance of their responsibility — without minimizing, without blame-shifting, and without excuse — for the evil someone else has suffered as a result of their sin choice.

Now, we need to note that there are many instances in the Bible where, even though God forgave the sins of a person or of the people, He did not remove the consequences of their sin (David, 2 Samuel 12:7-13; Children of Israel, Numbers 14:20-23). This means that while forgiveness is available, forgiveness does not mean "absence of consequences."

Repent: Repentance is more than a "change of mind;" it is a change of heart and of direction. Ephesians 4:28 gives us one of the best examples in Scripture of the "put off/put on" characteristics of authentic repentance:

> *"The one who steals must steal no longer; rather he must labor, doing good with his own hands, so that he may have something to share with the one who has need."*

Not only does the offender cease from doing bad, but he also replaces the unrighteous behavior with the opposite righteous behavior (direction change) – and continues doing so *over time* – and does so for the good of another (heart change).

> We also need to keep in mind that <u>there are two types of sorrow and shame for sin</u> (2 Corinthians 7:10); one is remorse, the other is regret.

2. **Internal Forgiveness**: This is where we extend mercy to the person who has wronged us, such that we completely forsake retaliation and revenge, leaving that person in the hands of God. Our best plans for revenge will fall far short of what God has planned because He seeks His righteous justice, not revenge. He *does* have a plan and we can trust Him in that (See Genesis 50:20).

Forsaking personal revenge does *not* mean, however, that the person who has wronged us is not held accountable for their actions, nor does it mean that we stuff our emotions about what happened and ignore them. That will set us on a downward spiral into the same destructive lies we have been working to become free from.

This level of forgiveness is almost impossible unless we have already gone to God and received His Judicial Forgiveness for ourselves.

Experiencing Judicial Forgiveness ourselves provides the seedbed for us to forgive others. Consider this: If God's forgiveness of us is not the foundation of our forgiveness of others, then we are, in actuality, establishing our own standards and patterns for forgiveness.

In such a scenario, we expect other people to live up to a standard for forgiveness that we have set in our own hearts. The sin issue at stake then becomes a matter between them and us, and not, as it ought to be, an issue between them and God. We have to be able to say, "This matter of sin stands between them (the other person) and God, based on His standards, and not between them and me, based on my standards.

When we live in unforgiveness, it is like carrying a backpack full of sharp, jagged rocks. We tote them around constantly. While we may learn to live with the pain and discomfort, our lives lack joy and God's peace. By contrast, when we forgive, we remove those jagged rocks and hand them over to God.

We walk away from them and leave them where they belong. Walking in unforgiveness means trying to bear something that is not ours to bear. Let that person be God's business, not yours. Romans 12:19: Leave room for the wrath of God ("Leave it to Me," says God).

3. **Relational Forgiveness:** God does not forgive relationally – we are not reconciled to or united with God – without confession and repentance on our part. Similarly, He does not require or even allow us to forgive others relationally without confession and repentance by the offending party (1 John 1:9; Luke 3:8).

This means that our ability to extend relational forgiveness to another person depends on their complete agreement as to the exact nature and character of their wrong (the meaning of the Biblical word "confess"). It also means that such forgiveness depends on those who have wronged us investing much energy and effort to "bear fruit in keeping with repentance" (Matthew 3:8; Ephesians 4:22, 24, 28).

When we speak here of another person confessing and repenting, we do not mean a mere change of behavior. Rather, confession and repentance that allows relational forgiveness flows from a change of heart. *The heart attitude is the key.*

It is the necessary ingredient underlying real change – change in which fruitful behavior replaces old toxic and sinful behavior. Such change takes time to prove itself genuine (Note: By way illustration, imagine a newly planted apple tree. We have to wait from 3 to 5 years for it to produce fruit – and the first crop is usually bitter).

Someone saying, "I'm sorry," is not confession, neither is it repentance, nor has there been any time for fruit to develop. Someone saying, "I'm really, *really* sorry," is neither confession nor repentance either.

A helpful parallelism for understanding the contrast between the prerequisites for

FORGIVENESS: It May Not Work the Way You Think

forgiveness and the prerequisites for reunion (Relational Forgiveness) can be found in Lewis Smedes', *The Art of Forgiving*: [2]

> *It takes one person to forgive.*
> *It takes two to be reunited.*
>
> *Forgiving happens inside the wounded person.*
>
> *Reunion happens in a relationship between people.*
>
> *We can forgive a person who never says he is sorry.*
>
> *We cannot be truly reunited unless he is honestly sorry.*
>
> *We can forgive even if we do not trust the person who wronged us once not to wrong us again.*
>
> *Reunion can happen only if we can trust the person who wronged us once not to wrong us again.*
>
> *Forgiving has no strings attached.*
> *Reunion has several strings attached.*

---

[2] Lewis Smedes, *The Art of Forgiving: When You Need to Forgive and Don't Know How* (Nashville, TN: Moorings, 1996), 27.

> **TRUE REPENTANCE IS:**
>
> - A GRIEVING OVER THE SINS ONE HAS COMMITTED;
>
> - A FULL AND OPEN ACCEPTANCE OF THE RESPONSIBILITY FOR THE EVIL SUFFERED BY THOSE WE HAVE WRONGED;
>
> - A COMPREHENSIVE FORSAKING OF THOSE SINS AND ANYTHING THAT MAKES THAT SIN EASY TO RECOMMIT;
>
> - AND A REPLACING OF THE SINFUL ATTITUDE AND BEHAVIOR WITH THE OPPOSITE RIGHTEOUS ATTITUDE AND BEHAVIOR, ALL *FOR THE SAKE OF GOD AND OTHERS* (SEE EPHESIANS 4:28).

The Bible teaches us that knowing the truth will set us free. It is hard for us to practice good until we know what *is* good. Once we have recognized and accepted the truth, then we are free to practice it.

A person who does not know the truth is like someone blind in a strange place. That person stumbles around, never sure of themselves, and is always lost.

Confession and repentance depend on truth, because they require a conviction that what we have done has violated *God's* moral code. Authentic confession and repentance do not come simply because we wish to avoid consequences.

For most of us, the first step to God's forgiveness has to be a willingness to internally forgive those who have wronged us. We must not continue in unforgiveness, knowing that this is a path to self-destruction.

A Truth in Love Biblical Counseling Resource

What About Forgiving Myself?

Some object to the idea of a person "forgiving themselves." The most common argument against this idea is that the Bible never mentions anyone forgiving themselves; it only speaks of God forgiving people and people forgiving each other. While this is technically correct, it is not entirely correct.

The assumption that we should not forgive ourselves is based on *technical theology*, not *practical theology*. *Technical theology* is a theology that can be supported with specific words and phrases in passages of Scripture.

Practical theology is how we live out our understanding of God and His Word. *Practical theology* is often a "real-life" application of *technical theology*, based on wisdom.

We could point to multiple examples of beliefs and convictions held true by Christians throughout history that derive not so much from an explicit statement of Scripture as from a wise application of the Bible to life.

In other cases, the descriptive portions of Scripture help us to understand God's ways apart from direct commands. In either case, that which we wisely discern from God's Word in partnership with the Holy Spirit we understand to be true and binding on our lives.

When it comes to "self-forgiveness," *practical theology* matters. To forgive ourselves is a matter of practicing for ourselves what we discern in the Bible about forgiveness.

We need to apply the same principles we have been discussing in this booklet: Are you holding yourself responsible and accountable for something that you are not responsible for, something for which God has already forgiven you in His Judicial Forgiveness?

If so, then you need to apply the principles of Internal Forgiveness to yourself.

To internally forgive someone who has harmed you in their sin means to surrender that person and their sin to God, since He is the only true and rightful Judge. When we feel like we cannot forgive ourselves, we must do the same.

We must surrender any judgment, condemnation, and expectation of vengeance against ourselves to God (1 Corinthians 4:3-4).

To refuse internal forgiveness to ourselves is, essentially, to declare that our moral standard is the ultimate moral standard of righteousness. This puts us in opposition to God. It puts us in the position where (in our minds and hearts) we take God's place as Judge and Savior. This prevents us from receiving and walking in God's forgiveness on every level.

So, if someone says you have no business talking about forgiving yourself, it may be simply because they do not understand the practical theology of forgiveness.

What About Being a Peacemaker?

Jesus encourages His followers (which includes us) that we will both be blessed by Him and give evidence that we are truly children of God if we live as peacemakers (Matthew 5:9).

What does it mean to be a peacemaker? How does that relate to our conversation about forgiveness?

It is important for us to understand the significant difference between "peacemaking" and "peace-faking."[3]

Peacemaking begins with the truth, understood and developed from our understanding of the nature and character of Jesus Christ, then fleshed-out in speaking that truth in love (Ephesians 4:15) without compromise.

Pacifying and placating are *not* **peacemaking**—they are **peace-faking** and begin with a denial of the truth of what has

---

[3] Concept introduced by Ken Sande in "The Peacemaker: A Biblical Guide to resolving Personal Conflict." (Baker Books, 1991). It is a recurring theme covered in their training program as well.

happened and what is happening, who is responsible for what, and pretending the problem does not exist—or running from the problem altogether.

Peacemaking is rooted and grounded in the truth and pursues putting an end to hostilities in a manner that is biblically consistent and honoring to God and the parties involved.

Peace-faking is rooted and grounded in avoiding the truth and the healthy confrontation that can result and seeks to pause the hostilities without resolution or reconciliation.

As we have discussed already, our own peace with God is based on facing and speaking the truth honestly to the Lord, who is Himself the Truth personified (John 14:6), and accepting the forgiveness that He grants as we confess ("speak the same truth the He does") our sin from a contrite and repentant heart.

To "forgive, forget, and move on" without God's prescription for forgiveness is peace-faking, NOT peacemaking.

Final Thoughts

It is God's desire that we understand the important teachings of the Bible so that we can enjoy the right relationship with Him that He originally intended for us.

One of those teachings is this one on **FORGIVENESS**.

<u>Without</u> His forgiveness through Jesus Christ, there would be no real hope for any of us.

<u>With</u> His forgiveness, there is everlasting hope for any of us who will accept His gift (free, no-cost-to-you, paid-in-full) that is ours when we place our trust in Jesus instead of whoever or whatever we have been trusting for peace, happiness, life, joy, and — more importantly — what our eternity will be.

Come to Him with the **contrite heart** we talked about.

Confess your selfish mutiny against His rightful place as King over your life.

And **repent** of the choices you have made (and still make) that oppose His moral code and His mandates for life. Ask His help in walking faithfully with Him. Repeat this as often as you need to. He will *always* forgive the contrite heart that turns to Him in true confession (1 John 1:9).

Then, extend the **forgiveness** you have received from God to those in your life who have wronged you (see Ephesians 4:32, our opening verse, and Matthew 6:14-15).

And remember to **walk forgiven**, even when you don't "feel" like it. The truth of God's forgiveness in Christ has nothing to do with whether or not we *feel* forgiven.

"Walking forgiven" keeps us focused forward instead of staring in the rearview mirror of our life and regretting what Christ has paid for and redeemed us from.

May God richly bless you as you learn to live forgiven and forgiving!"

Soli Deo Gloria

FORGIVENESS: It May Not Work the Way You Think

A Prayer of Surrender[4]

"Almighty God, I know and am fully convinced that I have sinned against You and that I deserve Your wrath. I also know and am fully convinced that, because of what Jesus did out of His love for me, I do not have to face that wrath.

I have chosen more than once to be the master of my own life and to live in ways I know are wrong. Please help me as I forsake that way of life. I know that Christ died for my sin, taking Your wrath for my sin on Himself so that I would never have to bear it. Thank you for offering that gift of mercy and grace. Thank you for providing full forgiveness for me through Jesus.

I also know that Jesus rose from death and wants to be Master of my life. I invite Him to take charge of my life and surrender it completely to You. In exchange, I gratefully receive Your gift of everlasting life. My desire is to live for You and to serve You, no matter what.

I know, too, that every area of my life now belongs to Jesus. Help me surrender more and more Each day bringing every thought, word, and deed into obedience to the truth that is in Him.

You are preparing a place for me with You, and I will one day be with You for the rest of eternity. Thank You for that wonderful promise and hope. In Jesus' name. Amen."

---

[4] *Unbound*, page 30.

ANCHOR POINTS

- God is the Author and Source of all forgiveness.
- Forgiveness is a matter of the heart and the will.
- In God's economy, consequences are often a part of the transaction, even when confession, repentance, and forgiveness take place. Forgiveness does not equal no consequences.
- Believers are to have hearts that tend toward forgiveness, but it is a forgiveness that needs to be Biblical in its formulation and execution.
- There are three types of forgiveness, the responsibility for which is mostly mine in only one instance.
- Internal and Relational Forgiveness are *not* synonymous. One does not necessarily lead to the other.
- God does not require or allow for Relational Forgiveness without specific prerequisites first being met.
- God does not expect us to forgive relationally until the offending party has done their part. The restoration of relationship is not a simple affair and must be done in accordance with God's directives.
- Inappropriate forgiveness puts us at odds with God. Appropriate forgiveness puts us in partnership with God.
- Apology-making is NOT forgiveness-seeking.

FORGIVENESS: It May Not Work the Way You Think

A Truth in Love Biblical Counseling Resource

For more information about the curriculum the material for this booklet comes from, visit
UnboundAndSetFree.com

The curriculum itself is available on Amazon as
Unbound: Growing Ever-Freer in Christ

To learn more about our counseling ministry
AuthenticBiblicalCounseling.com

For more information about training and equipping for discipleship and soul-care
TILBCC.com

We welcome your feedback via email
Admin@TILBCC.com

Made in the USA
Middletown, DE
19 July 2023

34838661R10021